Johnson's®

baby &
child safety

London, New York, Munich, Melbourne, Delhi

Text by Katy Holland

Senior editors Julia North, Salima Hirani
Project editor Anne Esden
Senior art editor Hannah Moore
Project art editor Tracy Miles
DTP designer Karen Constanti
Production controller Heather Hughes
Managing editors Anna Davidson, Liz Coghill
Managing art editor Glenda Fisher
Photography art direction Sally Smallwood
Photography Ruth Jenkinson

Publishing director Corinne Roberts

First published in Great Britain in 2004 by
Dorling Kindersley, A Penguin Company
80 Strand, London WC2R 0RL

A CIP catalogue record for this book is available from the British Library

ISBN 1 4053 0435 9

Reproduced by Colourscan, Singapore
Printed by Star Standard, Singapore

See our complete catalogue at
www.dk.com

A message to parents from
Johnson's®

The most precious gift in the world is a new baby. To your little one, you are the centre of the universe. And by following your most basic instincts to touch, hold and talk to your baby, you provide the best start to a happy, healthy life.

Our baby products encourage parents to care for and nurture their children through the importance of touch, developing a deep, loving bond that transcends all others.

Parenting is not an exact science, nor is it a one-size-fits-all formula. For more than a hundred years, Johnson & Johnson has supported the healthcare needs of parents and healthcare professionals, and we understand that all parents feel more confident in their role when they have information they can trust.

That is why we offer this book as our commitment to you to provide scientifically sound, professionally reviewed guidance on the important topics of pregnancy, babycare and child development.

As you read through this book, the most important thing to remember is this: you know your baby better than anyone else. By watching, listening and having confidence in your natural ability, you will know how to use the information you have in your hands, for the benefit of the baby in your arms.

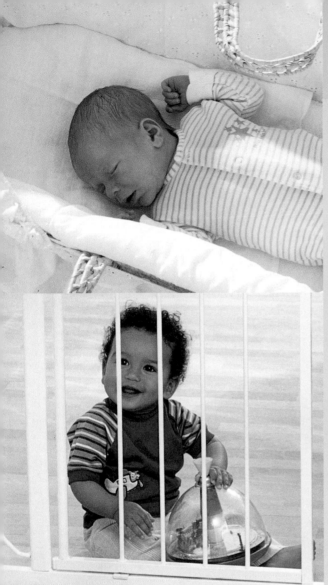

Contents

" Cara's **found her feet** and there's no stopping her! We've **made rooms safe** for her but, even so, she does bump herself now and again, especially when she's tired. "

PAMELA is mum to 17-month-old Cara

1

Your child's safety

Whether your child has just learned to roll over or climb his first tree, each developmental milestone brings feelings of pride and fulfilment to you both. At the same time, every new skill your child masters brings with it its own set of safety rules. So, throughout his early childhood, you will need to be one step ahead of him at all times to maintain these rules – and keep him safe.

From the moment he's born, your baby is instinctively curious. His immediate environment is an endless source of fascination, and he will be eager to explore it. This curiosity is part of his development – through touching, tasting and experimenting in different ways, he is taking in information that will help him master crucial life skills. But, during the early years, he has no concept of safety and his curiosity may lead to accidents.

Your young baby

Although your newborn can't move around on his own, remember that even young babies can wriggle, kick, grab things – and there is a first time for everything!

Keeping your young baby safe

● Use two hands when you carry him, and keep floors and stairs clear.

● Use a sling whenever you are carrying him outside.

● Never leave your baby on a high surface – not even for a minute.

● Keep furry pets away when he is sleeping, as they can suffocate him.

● Have a safe place to put him down in the living area of the house. A carrycot, playpen or baby seat is ideal.

● Never go near your baby with a hot drink in your hand.

● Keep him away from strings, from curtains or blinds or anything hanging that he may be able to grab.

Your mobile baby

Once your baby is able to roll over (any time after three months), you will need to take extra safety precautions. From as early as four months, he will be able to pull himself up, and he will soon start to move around. He will also want to

Individuality

Every child is unique and, to some extent, your child's temperament will determine his vulnerability to accidents.

● If he is extremely active or unusually curious, your child will probably be more at risk of injuring himself, so you will need to be extra cautious.

● At certain stages of development, he is likely to be stubborn, easily frustrated, aggressive or unable to concentrate – all characteristics associated with causing an injury.

● If you notice that your child is having a bad day, or going through a difficult phase, try to be especially alert, as this is when he is most likely to test safety rules, even those he usually follows.

Checklist

Being aware of the most common causes of injury at each stage of your child's development may help to avoid accidents.

Birth to four months
- Burns from adults' hot drinks or scalding bath water.
- Falls from changing tables or out of infant seats.
- Injury when an adult who is carrying him trips or falls.

Up to 18 months
- Injuries from toys (sharp edges, strings, choking hazards).
- Highchair accidents.
- Falls against sharp corners.
- Cigarette burns, and burns from grabbing things, such as hot drinks.
- Cuts from breakables.
- Babywalker or pushchair accidents.

18 months to three years
- Climbing accidents.
- Ingestion of poison.
- Unguarded water hazards, such as pools, baths or ponds.
- Cuts.
- Exploring accidents from cupboards or falling furniture.

Pre-school to five years
- Falls from bikes or play equipment.
- Poisoning.
- Falls from windows.

put everything into his mouth, so poisoning and choking become potential hazards.

Once he is on the move, much of your time will be spent keeping a close eye on him. Although it's important even at this age to tell him when something is harmful, he is far too young to understand the significance of what you are saying.

At this stage, your baby cannot be wilfully disobedient – his memory isn't developed enough to recall your warning the next time he's attracted to a forbidden object or activity. He is testing and re-testing reality, and this is a normal way of learning.

Keeping your mobile baby safe
- Always strap him securely into his highchair, car seat and pushchair.
- Make sure his toys meet safety standards and are age-appropriate (see pages 28–35).
- Childproof your home, if you have not already done so (see pages 36–45).

Your independent toddler

Toddlers are known for their desire for independence, and this, coupled with a keen sense of curiosity, can make this stage potentially the most hazardous. Although your child's physical skills are quite advanced, they far exceed his understanding of the consequences of his actions. His

AND SHE'S OFF!
As her physical skills develop, you need to be especially vigilant. Many more potential hazards will be within her reach.

judgement may start to improve now, but his sense of danger isn't developed, and he lacks self-control to stop if he sees something he wants.

Keeping your toddler safe
- Regularly check the sturdiness and condition of his cot, highchair and all other equipment.
- Set a good example. Your child learns by copying so, if he sees you throwing things into the fire or standing on a chair to reach a high shelf, he will do the same.
- Lock away all household chemicals and medicines – he may soon be able to open even childproof lids.
- Remove flimsy furniture and ensure that heavier pieces are secure.

Your pre-school child

Between the ages of three and five, your child will begin to grasp concepts such as cause and effect (he flicks a switch and the light goes on, for example), and his increased awareness of the influence he has on his environment means that his powers of reasoning are developing.

This newly acquired knowledge will help him avoid dangerous situations, but he is not yet mature enough to understand the potential dangers of his actions. He will enjoy testing his own abilities and setting himself new challenges.

Keeping your pre-school child safe

● Use the consequences of unsafe behaviour to explain the rationale behind safety rules. If he hurts himself by falling off a chair he was climbing on, for example, explain that this is why you have a rule about climbing. By explaining why things are dangerous – "Don't run out into the road, because you could be hit by a car" – you will help your child begin to grasp the meaning behind your warnings. He is still too young to understand the full meaning of your explanations, but he is learning fast.

● Be consistent and repeat rules in simple terms so he learns that unsafe actions are always unacceptable.

FIRST STEPS
Those first tottering steps are magical. Help her keep a firm grip on potentially slippery floors with bare feet, or put her in socks with rubberized soles.

" Joshua is really inquisitive. He has to explore everything, and often gets himself into difficulty. I'm always on my guard but, luckily, he's had no serious injuries. "

RUTH is mum to 18-month-old Joshua

Questions & Answers

I never let my baby out of my sight, so why do I need to childproof my home?
In order to develop, your baby needs your encouragement, praise and undivided attention, and this is best provided in an environment in which the obvious hazards have been removed. Constantly saying "No!" or telling him off can leave him feeling negative about himself. It's far better

to allow him the freedom he needs to explore. If you feel relaxed, so will he, and his confidence will blossom.

It is true that with constant vigilance most injuries can be avoided. Your child requires your full attention when he is in your care, and he will need you to interact with him, guide him and direct him out of harm's way when necessary.

But even the most conscientious parent can't watch a child every moment. Most

injuries occur not when parents are alert and at their best, but when they are under stress – and everyone has moments like this.

Childproofing eliminates, or reduces, the opportunities for injury so that even when you are momentarily distracted, your child is less likely to encounter situations and objects that can cause him harm. For advice on how to childproof your home, see pages 36–45.

In the care of others

When you're leaving your baby or young child in the care of other people, whether on a regular or occasional basis, you want to be sure that he'll be well cared for. But other carers' homes may not be suitably childproofed, so it's your responsibility to check and point out potential hazards.

• **Childminders** By law, childminders must be registered with your local authority. This means that many basic safety checks will have been carried out. But even though a childminder is registered, it does not mean that her home is as safe as you might wish. It's important to ask her opinions about safety matters, and have a good look around her home and garden to satisfy yourself that it is a safe place for your child. If she's serious about childminding, she will not mind. Also, check that her registration and insurance documents are current.

• **Nurseries** Like childminders, nurseries are regularly inspected by local authorities to ensure they are meeting the requirements of the law and still worthy of their registration. You are entitled to a copy of their reports. However, some nurseries have higher safety standards than others, so it is vital that you check around the nursery yourself.

Expert tips

When you need a babysitter, it's best to pick someone you know. If you do advertise, however, always follow up references.

• Always leave a contact number with your babysitter. You could also leave the telephone number of your GP.

• Always introduce your child to a babysitter before deciding whether to leave him in his or her care.

• Show your babysitter where important items for your child are kept, and point out emergency exits.

• Don't ask your babysitter to bath your baby or child unless you have confidence in his or her ability to do so.

Emotional security

Keeping your child safe doesn't just mean protecting him from physical dangers. By giving him your love, support and encouragement, you are naturally providing him with everything he needs to become a confident and secure individual, who is not frightened of what life has to offer. Cuddles, kisses and praise go a long way, and the more generous you are with these, the better.

Your child will feel most secure when he is with you, and will thrive on the routines of your day-to-day life together. Studies show that babies, children and adults alike benefit from having a consistent, predictable pattern to their days. Regular mealtimes and bedtime rituals instill a sense of security, helping your child feel confident enough to explore and develop in his own way.

Of course, this does not mean sticking to a rigid timetable: routines and daily patterns should emerge naturally, and occasional changes, disruptions or new events can, and should, be welcomed.

SAFE IN YOUR LOVE
Babies and children grow confident and feel secure knowing that they are loved and valued by their parents.

" We bought the **best quality** cot we could afford for Benjamin. It's solidly built and easy to use. He's only tiny now, but we have a feeling he's going to be quite **boisterous** as he gets bigger! "

TONY is dad to four-month-old Benjamin

Sleeping safely

Parents often worry more about their babies when they are asleep than when they are awake, particularly during the first few months of life. But, by taking sensible precautions and following the recommended advice, you can relax, knowing that your baby is as safe as possible while she sleeps.

Whether she is sleeping in a Moses basket next to your bed, or a cot or bed in her own room, there are a number of safety issues to consider.

Moses baskets

Many newborn babies prefer the smaller space of a Moses basket to a cot. The carry handles allow you to transfer the basket between rooms (but you should never do this with your baby inside).

● When choosing a Moses basket, look for British Standard BS EN 1466.

● Make sure that the basket is firm and sturdy, with strong handles.

● Check that the mattress is a close fit (especially if you buy it separately). There should be no space between the edges of the mattress and the basket.

● Check that the stand fits your basket snugly. It's best to buy one that has been specifically designed to hold your particular basket.

● Once your baby reaches 6kg (13lb), begins to roll or simply looks as though she is becoming too big for the basket (usually by the age of three or four months), it's time to move her into a cot.

● Never carry your baby around in the Moses basket. Babies can slip out of them – particularly when being carried up or down stairs.

Cradles

Rocking cradles are a cosy fit and can be soothing for young babies. Like Moses baskets, they are suitable for use from newborn until your baby can sit up, kneel or roll over

SWEET DREAMS
A Moses basket is very practical in the early weeks. Keep it by your bedside to make night wakings and feeds easier.

Expert tips

Protect your sleeping baby by:

• placing her on her back with her feet to the foot of the Moses basket, cradle or cot (see page 16)

• dressing her in flame-resistant, snug-fitting sleepwear

• placing her away from windows, blinds or cords, and electrical items

• making sure household pets do not have access to her

• keeping her out of direct sunlight and away from radiators or heaters.

(usually around three or four months). Once your baby has the strength to pull herself up, you should stop using it immediately and move her into a cot.

• The cradle should be on a firm stand and any rocking mechanism should be lockable.

• Always make sure that the cradle is locked into a stationary position while your baby is sleeping, and that it cannot be tipped over.

• Ensure the mattress fits snugly all around the cradle sides, with no gaps that could trap your baby.

Cots

Your baby can sleep safely in a cot until she's at least 18 months old, and perhaps even up to two years or more. You'll know when she has outgrown it because she will start trying to climb out of it. That's the time to move her to a bed.

Falls are the most common injuries associated with cots but, fortunately, they are the easiest to prevent. Babies are most likely to fall out of their cot when the mattress is raised too high for their height, or when the side rail is left down.

Cot safety check

The following guidelines will ensure that your baby stays safe in her cot at all times.

• Cot bars should be no more than 6cm (2³/₈in) apart, to avoid your baby's head and limbs getting stuck.

• The distance between the top of the mattress and the top of the cot should be at least 50cm (20in) in the lowest position and 20cm (8in) in the highest position. Lower the mattress as your baby grows to a level where she cannot fall if she pulls herself up. Set the mattress at its lowest position by the time she can stand.

• There should be no horizontal bars or toys on your cot that could enable your baby to climb up.

• When you put your baby in the cot, always pull the side up and check that the drop-side mechanism is locked.

• Never use cot bumpers. They can cause overheating (see page 16), and they can also be used to climb on.

• Hang mobiles securely and well out of reach. Remove them when your baby is able to get up on her hands and knees, or when she reaches the age of five months, whichever is soonest.

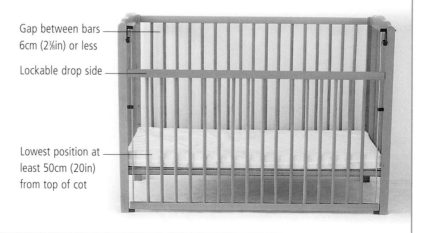

Gap between bars 6cm (2⅜in) or less

Lockable drop side

Lowest position at least 50cm (20in) from top of cot

FEET TO FOOT
Placing babies to sleep with their feet to the foot of the cot has been found to reduce significantly the risk of SIDS (see below).

of the sides or ends of the mattress and the cot frame. Keep your baby's mattress well-aired and clean.

● **Mattress base height** Most cot mattress bases have adjustable levels. You start with the mattress at the highest setting for easy access to your baby, and then lower it as she grows (see page 14).

● **Castors** Ensure that these are lockable – an energetic baby could easily make the cot move around.

Concern over SIDS

All parents worry about the possibility of cot death, or Sudden Infant Death Syndrome (SIDS), but it is important to remember that the chances of it happening to your baby are unlikely.

The causes of this tragic syndrome are not yet fully understood, but there are some important precautions you can take that will significantly reduce the risk.

The following recommendations apply throughout your baby's first year, although they are particularly important during the first six months, when incidences of SIDS are at their highest. If your baby sleeps while being cared for by a babysitter

Make sure your baby's cot is safety approved. Modern cots are required by law to meet certain safety standards (see page 14). Look for standard BS EN 716. If you buy a new cot of this standard, you can be sure that it will have been designed so that your baby cannot easily fall out or injure herself in any way on the cot.

When choosing a cot, you should consider the following points.

● **Sturdiness** A cot will inevitably end up as an early-morning playpen once your baby is able to sit up and move around, so make sure it can take the strain. All screws and bolts must be tightly in place to prevent the cot from coming apart.

● **Drop sides** One or both of the cot sides should drop for easy access. The drop-side mechanism

needs to be very sturdy because you will soon have a baby who can jump up and down and rattle the bars. Look for a mechanism that can be operated with one hand if possible, as you will invariably have your baby in your other arm when you come to use it.

● **Teething rails** Once she can stand, your baby will probably want to try out her new teeth on the top of her cot. Plastic strips along the edge will protect her from splinters.

● **The mattress** Mattresses are made of foam or natural fibres. Either is fine to use, as long as it is firm, not soft, it doesn't sag, and shows no sign of deterioration. Look for a cot mattress that is made to BS 1877 and BS 7177, and the correct size for the cot. You should not be able to slide two fingers between any

Questions & Answers

Should I let my new baby fall asleep in his car seat?

Newborn babies do seem to settle well in their car seats, perhaps because they can adopt a more curled-up position. However, the safest sleeping position for your baby is on his back, on a firm mattress.

Although it is safe for him to fall asleep in his car seat during the day if he is within your sight, you should never put him down for the night in it. Always ensure that his head is supported in his car seat by the padded car seat head rest. If he's allowed to slump over with his head down, it can restrict his breathing and be dangerous.

When your baby is in his car seat, never be tempted to put it on a high surface, as it could topple – seats falling from high surfaces are a common cause of accidents for babies.

" It's hard not to keep checking on Charlie when he's sleeping. Often he seems so still and his breathing so shallow, I can't resist touching or stroking him to make him stir a little. "

CHIARA is mum to two-month-old Charlie

or grandparent, or anyone else, make sure they also follow these guidelines.

- **Put your baby down to sleep on her back** Studies have proved that back sleeping, rather than tummy sleeping, significantly lowers the risk of SIDS, although the reasons for this remain unclear. Once your baby is older, she will be able to turn onto her tummy by herself – don't worry about this. Just continue to put her down to sleep on her back when you first put her to bed.
- **Never smoke around your baby, and keep her well away from smoky atmospheres** Babies who are exposed to cigarette smoke are at a higher risk of dying from SIDS.
- **Make sure your baby's bedroom is the right temperature – around 18°C (65°F)** Overheating can be life-threatening to your baby and is known to have a strong link with SIDS. Your baby's body is not mature enough to regulate its own temperature properly; she cannot sweat if she gets too hot.

- **Place her with her feet at the foot of the Moses basket, cradle or cot** This is very important, mainly because it allows your baby to wriggle free from her bedclothes if she becomes overheated.
- **Never use duvets or quilts** These can cause your baby to become overheated. Use a sheet or one or two layers of thin cellular blankets, which are tucked in at the sides and the foot of the mattress, no higher than your baby's chest. In warmer weather, remove a layer or take off the bedding altogether.
- **Never use cot bumpers** These can contribute to overheating, and can also restrict breathing if your baby becomes entangled in them. For similar reasons, do not give your baby a pillow or leave soft toys in her Moses basket, cradle or cot, and never put her to sleep on a cushion, beanbag or waterbed.
- **Don't use hot water bottles or electric blankets** These can cause overheating or scalding.
- **Use a firm mattress** You should also make sure there is no gap between the mattress edges and the sides of the cot (see pages 14–15).

A BABY MONITOR
A monitor allows you to hear your baby from elsewhere in your home whenever he stirs in his cot. It can help satisfy you that he's safe and settled without the need to keep checking on him.

● **Seek medical advice promptly** If you suspect that your baby is unwell, call your doctor immediately.

Your baby's breathing

It's only natural to worry about your baby's breathing while she sleeps. Many parents pay frequent visits to their sleeping babies to check on them. This can do no harm, but it's important not to become over-anxious about it.

Bear in mind that your baby's breathing will often be irregular, and that her breathing patterns will vary while she sleeps. When she is in dream (REM) sleep, she will breathe

quite quickly, grunting and twitching a lot. The rest of her sleep will be deeper and quieter, and she may be so still that it will be hard to tell if she is breathing without touching her. As your baby grows, and you get to know her, you will become less panicky about her breathing. A baby monitor will enable you to listen in to her normal snuffles and grunts, as well as alert you when she's crying, and should give you peace of mind.

Breathing monitors

These sensitive devices register your baby's breathing using ultrasound beams or electronic pads that go

Medical help

Consult your doctor or health visitor if:

● your baby or child appears to have difficulty breathing or snores frequently

● your baby is sick or feverish

● your baby or child has persistent difficulties sleeping

● your baby or child suddenly starts having unusual night wakings

● your baby or child wakes up coughing throughout the night

● an allergy, such as eczema, is affecting her sleep.

MOVING TO A BIG BED
When your child is ready to move to a bed, a bed guard, which can be raised and lowered as needed, will prevent her from falling out.

under the mattress or on your baby's tummy. An alarm sounds if there is a significant pause (around 20 seconds) in your baby's breathing.

Health professionals usually advise using them only in special cases – for example, if there is a known underlying health problem or a history of SIDS in the family.

Whether such instruments offer reassurance in normal circumstances is debatable. While some parents find they reduce anxiety, others find that they serve only to increase their worries because of the many inevitable false alarms.

The Foundation for the Study of Infant Deaths (see page 62) says that it is far better to know and practise preventative methods for dealing with SIDS than to use electronic breathing monitors.

From cot to bed

When your child is ready for a bed, consider using a mattress on the floor to begin with until she gets used to it. Then fit a safety-approved guard rail to the bed to stop her falling out.

If the bed is against a wall, ensure there's no gap in which she could get trapped. You may also want to fit a stair gate across her room at night, to prevent her from going downstairs without you, for example.

Bunk bed safety

Children may love them, but bunk beds can be hazardous. Falls from top bunks are a common cause of accidents, and children on lower bunks can (and do) become injured by collapsing top bunks.

If you choose to use bunk beds, the following guidelines will help:

• Ensure there is no gap between mattresses and the bed frames.

• Place beds in the corner of the room (away from windows) so that there are walls on two sides. This gives extra support and decreases the risk of falling out.

• Don't allow a child under the age of six years to sleep in the top bunk bed.

• Attach a ladder to the top bunk, and keep a night light on so that your child can see it.

• The top bunk must have a guard rail on all sides. The gap between the bed and guard rail should be no more than 9cm (3½in) wide. Check that your child can't roll under the rail when her mattress is compressed by her body weight.

• Check that mattresses are well supported. Wires or slats should run directly under and be secured at both ends. A mattress that is held only by the frame can come crashing down on to the bunk below.

• Never allow your children to jump on the bunks.

Is it safe to share my bed with my baby?

Bed-sharing – or co-sleeping – has practical and emotional advantages, and many parents do choose this option. However, before you decide to sleep with your baby in your bed, it is important to be aware of the potential safety hazards.

Although co-sleeping is generally considered to be safe if certain guidelines are followed, some studies have linked it with a higher risk of SIDS. A good alternative is to place your baby's Moses basket or cot next to your bed or opt for a specially designed bedside cot that has a removable side, so it becomes an extension of your bed.

Having said that, co-sleeping is a personal – and sometimes cultural – choice. So if you do decide it is for you, follow these essential safety precautions.

★ **Keep babies under the age of eight weeks out of the family bed** Studies have linked co-sleeping with an increased risk of SIDS in this age group.

★ **Never co-sleep if you or your partner smoke** Again, this has been linked with SIDS (see page 16).

★ **Never sleep with your baby if either of you have recently drunk alcohol** Also avoid it if you are taking medication that causes drowsiness.

★ **Remove all padded bedding** That includes duvets and pillows, and give your baby space or she could be squashed or fall out of the bed.

★ **Make sure your mattress is firm** Soft mattresses, waterbeds and beanbags are not safe.

★ **Ideally, put your mattress on the floor** If not, it must fit tightly against the headboard and wall.

★ **Dress your baby lightly** Also, you should not use heavy blankets or thick sheets.

★ **Never let anything cover your baby's head** Keep blankets no higher than her chest level.

★ **Never sleep with your baby on a sofa**.

SAFE TOGETHER
Co-sleeping can be a rewarding experience for both you and your baby, but you must follow all the necessary safety advice.

"Gabriel really tucks in to his **finger foods**. I always keep a close eye on him in case he **bites off** more than he can chew!"

MARIA is mum to 12-month-old Gabriel

Eating safely

Every parent knows that keeping your baby healthy means feeding him the right foods as part of a well-balanced diet, but it's also important that you prepare his food hygienically and sterilize his feeding equipment to ensure that he doesn't get a stomach upset or, worse, food poisoning.

Sterilizing

It is important to sterilize all your baby's feeding equipment for the first six months to prevent any bacterial contamination.

Before sterilizing, make sure that you wash everything (bottles, neck rings, teats and tops) separately in hot, soapy water, using a bottle brush and teat cleaner.

Rinse well, and either leave to drain, or dry with a clean tea towel or paper towel. Germs thrive on used and wet tea towels, so avoid these when drying your baby's feeding equipment.

There are three ways of sterilizing:

● Boiling

Bring a large pan of water to the boil and immerse all the bottle parts fully, making sure there are no air pockets in the bottle itself. Cover the pan and leave to boil for 10 minutes.

You can leave the bottle parts in the covered pan until you are ready to use them again. Alternatively, remove them and dry them with a clean towel.

Boiling is the simplest and cheapest method of sterilizing, but repeated boiling can make teats sticky, and bottles tend to go cloudy. When this happens, they should be replaced.

● Steam sterilizers

With an electric steamer, you simply add the recommended amount of water and switch on. A microwave steam sterilizer works in much the same way – a cupful of water is added to the base of the sterilizer, which is then placed in the microwave for about 10 minutes.

● Sterilizing liquid or tablets

Using a large container filled with water, add the recommended number of tablets or amount of fluid and totally immerse the equipment, making sure there are no air bubbles. Leave for about 30 minutes. Rinse with cooled, boiled water before use.

Expert tips

● Use clean, dry cloths or paper towels for drying up. Germs multiply on damp cloths and tea towels.

● Clean all kitchen surfaces, highchair, refrigerator door handle, bin lid etc, regularly to minimize bacteria growth. Thoroughly rinse kitchen cloths and sponges after use, and hang out to dry.

● Always wash your hands before making up your baby's feeds or preparing his food.

● Keep pets away from areas where you prepare food. Never let cats walk on work surfaces or table tops, as they can pass on lethal bacteria, as well as infections, such as toxoplasmosis (see page 52).

How can I prepare my child's food safely?

Basic food hygiene is essential for everyone – but especially for babies and young children who may be more susceptible to infection. Following these simple rules on food safety and hygiene each time you prepare a meal will ensure that your child stays in the best of health.

Preparation and cooking

★ **Always wash your hands thoroughly before preparing your child's food** Germs can be picked up from anywhere – the supermarket, your car, around the house, when changing nappies or from stroking animals. Use warm, soapy water to kill off any bacteria, sweeping over the backs of your hands as well as your palms. Dry your hands carefully, using a clean, dry towel.

★ **Wash fruit, vegetables and meat before preparation or cooking** All these food items will have been handled by someone else before reaching the supermarket shelves. This is why it is important always to rinse well and pat dry before preparing. For babies, fruit and vegetables should always be peeled as well as washed.

★ **Always use different chopping boards for meat and vegetables** Making sure that you keep separate chopping boards for the preparation of meat and vegetables will help to prevent cross-contamination of bacteria. Plastic chopping boards are more hygienic, easier to clean and less likely to harbour bacteria in grooves made by knife blades than wooden ones.

★ **Cook food thoroughly** Always cook meat, fish and poultry well to kill off bacteria and parasites. Meat that has not been cooked thoroughly can be a source of salmonella or listeria food poisoning. To check that meat is cooked properly, stick a skewer or knife into the centre. If it is ready, the juices should run clear.

★ **Avoid microwaving your baby's food or milk** Microwave ovens create hot spots, which can burn your baby's mouth.

★ **Always test the temperature of food before offering it to your baby** Your baby has a very sensitive mouth that will burn easily. Test the temperature of the food against your arm or with a fingertip. Slightly warm is best for your baby.

Storing food safely

★ **Don't keep half-used jars of baby food** If you use pre-prepared baby foods, always transfer how much you think your baby will eat into a bowl rather than feed him straight from the jar, as leftovers will be contaminated with his saliva. Throw away leftovers within 24 hours. Never use a jar if it appears to have been opened before, and always check "sell-by" and "use-by" dates.

★ **Store food in sealed containers or cover with cling wrap before putting it in the fridge** This will help prevent food from becoming contaminated by bacteria. Don't give your baby any food that has been left in the fridge for more than 24 hours. Raw meat should be stored in a sealed container in the bottom of the fridge to prevent any juices dripping onto cooked foods.

★ **Never re-freeze any cooked food that has already been frozen once** This is particularly true for any meat that has been frozen before, as freezing it again can cause bacterial contamination.

WASH YOUR HANDS
To protect your child's health, it's important to get into the habit of washing your hands with soap and drying them on a clean cloth or paper towel before you prepare food. You should also wash your hands after handling food, particularly raw meat.

VEGETABLE PREPARATION
Vegetables and fruit should always be thoroughly washed before preparation to kill off bacteria and rinse away any pesticide residues. To give your baby extra protection, peel all vegetables and fruit before serving.

Food intolerances

If your child suffers a reaction to a food, it is likely to be because of an intolerance, which means that his digestive system is having difficulty breaking down certain foods. Lactose intolerance, for example, which is common in children, is the inability to digest the sugars in cow's milk, and occurs because the enzyme lactase is missing from the digestive tract.

Unlike an allergy, which produces a swift reaction, a food intolerance may contribute to conditions, such as:

- asthma
- eczema
- diarrhoea
- constipation
- hives
- stomach pains
- behavioural problems (intolerance has been linked with Attention Deficit Hyperactivity Disorder or ADHD).

Allergies

True food allergies are quite rare. An allergy occurs when the body's immune system immediately reacts to a substance (or allergen) as if it were harmful. It responds by producing an antibody, which triggers the release of histamine as a defence, causing the symptoms associated with an allergy. Symptoms of allergy can include:

- asthma or wheezing

Questions & Answers

What should I do if my child has an allergic reaction?
Common foods that trigger intolerances or allergic reactions include: wheat, dairy products, strawberries, shellfish, nuts, baby formula and soya. If your child does suffer a reaction after eating a trigger food, **take him to your doctor or hospital immediately**.

A rare but severe reaction to a particular food is known as anaphylactic shock. Symptoms can include wheezing, swelling of the face, lips and throat, which leads to breathing problems as the airway is restricted, a rapid drop in blood pressure and loss of consciousness. You should take your child to hospital or call an ambulance without delay, as immediate treatment with adrenaline will be needed.

FOODS TO TREAT WITH CAUTION
Foods that commonly trigger allergies or food intolerances include egg whites, wheat, nuts and strawberries. Seek the advice of your health visitor or doctor before introducing any of these foods to your child's diet, especially if there is a history of allergies in your family.

Organic food

If you are worried about the levels of pesticide residues on food, you may feel it is a safer option to feed your baby organic food. The produce might not look as attractive in shape, size or colour as non-organic, but this is because it has been left to grow more naturally.

Ingredients that have a Soil Association certificate comply with strict organic regulations. Remember, however, that "organic" doesn't necessarily mean pesticide-, chemical- or antibiotic-free. Regulations allow for certain types of these chemicals to be used.

- shortness of breath
- sneezing
- blocked sinuses
- runny nose
- coughing
- swollen, itchy eyes, nose, palate, throat and lips
- diarrhoea or vomiting.

It has also been associated with ADHD.

What to do

If you think your child may be suffering from an intolerance or allergy, don't try to eliminate foods by yourself as you need to isolate the culprit without adversely affecting your child's diet. Seek guidance from your health

visitor or doctor, who may refer your child to a specialist.

If allergies run in your family it may be better to follow the list below as a general guide of when to introduce foods, to minimize the risk. Introduce foods one at a time so you can watch for any adverse reaction, but bear in mind that a reaction may not happen the first time your child is exposed to a food.

The following foods may be introduced earlier if there is no history in your family, but remember to introduce them one at a time.

- **Six to eight months** Fruit (except citrus), vegetables (except peppers, tomatoes), pulses, rice, beans, meat, poultry, fish (not shellfish), egg yolks.

- **Nine to 14 months** Corn, oats, live yogurt, potatoes, peppers, eggs, tomatoes, shellfish, soya products.
- **15+ months** Wheat, dairy products, seeds, oranges. Ground nuts and nut products can be introduced from the age of three years. However, don't give whole nuts until your child is at least seven years old because of the risk of choking (see page 27).

Choosing a highchair

Once your baby can sit up on his own (from about five months), he will need a highchair where he can sit safely during mealtimes. When buying one, look for British Standard BS 5799.

Highchair safety

● Never leave your baby alone in his highchair, no matter how securely you have strapped him in.

● As you slide the tray on, be careful of your baby's fingers and hands to prevent pinching.

● Keep the highchair at a safe distance from tables and worktops. Your child could tip the highchair over by pushing off with hands and feet.

● Ensure caps or plugs on tubing on metal highchair frames are firmly attached and cannot be pulled off and choke a child.

● If it is a folding highchair, it should have an effective locking device to prevent it collapsing.

● Always use a five-point harness; otherwise your child could slide under the tray and trap his neck.

● If using a hook-on chair, never place it where your child can push off with his feet.

A SAFE SEAT
Accidents involving highchairs are common, so it's vital to be safety conscious every time you use one.

Naturally, modern highchair manufacturers put safety first, but styles vary and it is important, for your own peace of mind, to take the time to carry out some basic safety checks before you buy.

● Look for a sturdy chair that will not easily topple once your child is sitting in it. The wider the base, the better – make sure it is between 48 and 64cm (19 and 25in) wide.

● The highchair should have a five-point harness to keep your child secure once strapped in. If you are buying the harness separately, look for British Standard BS 6684. A crotch strap alone is not sufficient to hold your baby securely. Remember to use the five-point harness every time you put your baby in the highchair – even if it is only for a minute.

● Mealtimes can be very messy, so it is important to choose a highchair with a seat and tray that are easy to keep clean and no awkward spots that could trap food.

There are a number of types of seats to choose from.

● **Wooden highchairs** are sturdy,

easy to wipe clean and will last well if you have more than one child. Many also convert into a table and chair once your child has outgrown the highchair.

● **Fold-away highchairs** come with padded seats and fold flat for easy storage. However, choose carefully when you buy – some are not as sturdy as others, and the wipe-clean fabric can deteriorate with wear and tear after prolonged use.

● **Booster seats** are useful for an older toddler who has outgrown his highchair. These can be strapped to any dining chair with an adaptable harness which fixes underneath and/or behind the chair. These seats are for children who feel confident about sitting at a table and who won't suddenly keel over sideways. Always fasten the straps securely before a child sits in the chair.

● **Clip-on seats** or seats that screw onto the table are useful at home if space is tight, when eating out in restaurants or when travelling. But some safety experts advise against using these because many surfaces are not strong enough to have a seat attached to them. If you do use one, look for standard BS EN 1272. Check that the table top is very strong, and the chair securely fastened.

A BOOSTER SEAT
Once he's outgrown his highchair, a booster seat can be strapped to an adult chair and brings your child right up to the table.

Choking

Choking can be caused by any small pieces of food or objects which block the airway. Half of all cases of choking in young children involve food, and the most common culprits are sweets, which account for around 32 per cent of all choking accidents. Other foods likely to cause choking include fish bones, biscuits and pieces of fruit.

The following are all signs that your baby or child could be choking.

● difficulty breathing

● flushed neck and face

● strange noises or no sound at all

● skin turning grey-blue.

To minimize the risk of choking:

● never leave your baby or child alone when he is eating

● never let your child run around with a toy or food in his mouth

● never give nuts, boiled sweets or small toys, which can easily cause choking

● always check toys for small removable parts

● follow manufacturers' guidelines about the suitability of age-appropriate toys.

What to do

Sadly, choking is a common cause of accidental death in babies and children under three years old, so it is vital to know what to do if your child starts to choke. It's a good idea to enroll in a first-aid course from a recognized organization, such as the British Red Cross, St John Ambulance or St Andrew's Ambulance Association (see page 62), so that you receive expert training on how to cope in all emergencies, including choking. Ask your health visitor or at your doctor's surgery for details of courses in your area.

" Phoebe's always putting things in her mouth, especially **her toys**. I do wash them from time to time but, more regularly, I check for **broken bits** and throw the toys away if I find any. **"**

KATE is mum to six-month-old Phoebe

4

Playing safely

For your child to develop the skills she needs in life, she will benefit from lots of playtime and stimulation. Providing her with safe toys and objects to experiment with, and giving her plenty of positive input, is the best way you can help her to do this. It's also of primary importance that she has somewhere safe to play.

There are many things you can do to make sure that your child plays safely. Toy and equipment manufacturers now have stringent safety guidelines, and most products are rigorously tested before they are marketed. However, it's still very important to be aware of potential hazards, whether you're choosing a new piece of nursery equipment or a toy to entertain your baby.

In the early months, it may be worth investing in one or two pieces of nursery equipment, such as a playpen or bouncy chair, where your baby can be stimulated in a happy and safe environment.

Playpens and travel cots

Playpens can be a temporary safe place in which to put your baby when you are not available to play with her. It should be emphasized, however, that you should always keep your baby within your sights, and that playpens are recommended for use only over short periods.

Many modern playpens double up as travel cots and are particularly useful if you are going to stay away from home. They are usually constructed from mesh material attached to a fold-away metal frame.

Although modern playpens are made according to strict safety guidelines, it's wise to follow these precautions.

• Always make sure that the playpen is erected properly, with all sides up. Never leave the side of a mesh playpen lowered as your baby could roll into the pocket created by the slack material and suffocate.

• As soon as your baby is able to sit up, remove any toys that have been attached to the playpen so that she cannot become entangled in them.

• As soon as she is able to stand, remove any large toys that she could use as a foothold to climb out.

Expert tips

Infants, toddlers and pre-school children should never be given toys with the following:

• electrical parts – anything that needs plugging into the mains

• parts that could be pulled off and swallowed and/or fit into a child's nose or ear

• exposed wires and parts that can get hot

• lead paint or other toxic materials (use non-toxic paints and crayons)

• breakable parts

• sharp points or edges

• glass or thin parts

• springs or hinges that can pinch tiny fingers or get caught in hair.

• Check mesh playpens regularly for tears and holes. Teething babies may bite the plastic coverings on the top rails, leaving rips which should be mended immediately with heavy-duty cloth tape.

• If you have a playpen with wooden bars, it is essential that the slats are no more than 6cm (2⅜in) apart so that your baby's head or limbs cannot become trapped between them.

Bouncy chairs

Before your baby is able to sit up unsupported, a bouncy chair is an ideal first seat for her. She'll probably far prefer this position to lying on her back, as it gives her a chance to see what's going on around her. Newer designs often have detachable bars to which you can attach toys.

• The chair seat should have a wide base, a sturdy, non-skid bottom and a crotch and waist safety strap.

• Make sure it has a firm back support, and use it only for short periods at a time.

• Always strap your baby in.

• Until your baby has good head control, always use a head support like those used in car seats.

• Never put your baby's seat on any high surface. Even a very young baby

" The playpen has come in handy when I've needed somewhere safe to put Isobel for a short while. I chat to her while she plays, and she soon lets me know when it's time to come out!"

SUSIE is mum to six-month-old Isobel

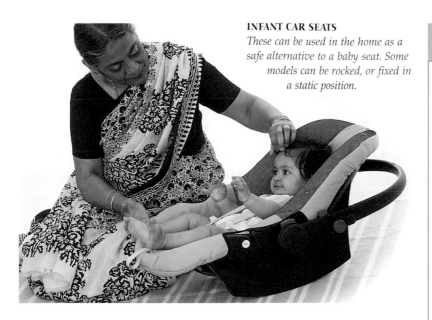

INFANT CAR SEATS
These can be used in the home as a safe alternative to a baby seat. Some models can be rocked, or fixed in a static position.

can kick and wriggle, which can cause the seat to move and perhaps topple off.

• Never try to strap your baby in one of these seats in the car. You should always use a car seat (see pages 56–57).

Door bouncers

Door bouncers attach to the top of a door frame, and your baby sits inside a padded fabric seat, which supports her body. The seat is suspended from a strong elasticated strap fixed by a spring-loaded clip attached to the door frame or a free-standing frame. Look out for door bouncers that have plastic or cushioned rings around them designed to prevent your baby from bumping into the frame.

• Your baby should only be put into a door bouncer when she has full control of her head (between the ages of three and five months), and you should stop using it when she has reached the recommended maximum weight (usually around 12kg/26lb) or when she shows signs of trying to walk.

• The length of the bouncer's straps should be adjusted so that your baby's feet just touch the floor.

• The bouncer should be used only for 15 to 20 minutes at a time.

• Ensure that the seat can be sufficiently adjusted to fit snugly around your baby and support her back, and always use the safety harness and straps.

• Never leave your baby in a door bouncer unattended.

Baby walkers

From around six months, many parents consider using baby walkers – wheeled devices that hold babies in an upright position with their feet on the floor.

Contrary to their name, baby walkers will not help your baby learn to walk. While they may strengthen the muscles in the lower legs, they don't stimulate or strengthen the upper legs or hips, which are the muscles that are used most in walking. Many experts believe these walkers are actually detrimental to development, as they can eliminate a baby's desire to try to walk independently.

Baby walkers are also a serious safety hazard. They can easily tip over, particularly when they bump into an obstacle such as a toy or rug. Children in baby walkers are far more likely to fall down stairs and get into dangerous places and situations that would otherwise be beyond their reach. For these reasons, baby walkers are *not* recommended by safety experts.

• Always make sure the door is wedged open.

• Be particularly vigilant when other children are around – they may be tempted to try to swing the baby in the bouncer or may inadvertently close the door on your baby, with disastrous results.

Questions & Answers

What should I look for when I'm choosing new toys for my baby?

By being aware of potential pitfalls when buying toys for your baby and practising a few simple rules for safe use, you can prevent injuries before they occur.

The golden rule is to always read the label on the packaging. This will give you important information about how to use a toy, what age baby or child it is safe for, and whether adult supervision is recommended. For infants, look for toys labelled as being suitable for children aged three and under, because government guidelines require that they have no small parts which could be swallowed or inhaled (see right).

In the UK, a toy that conforms to safety standards will carry the CE or Lion Mark on its label or packaging. Toys bearing these marks mean they have been tested rigorously. They also mean that a toy does not contain: dangerous chemicals (such as lead) in paint, sharp edges, flammable materials, electric plugs or any small parts that your child could choke on.

If a toy doesn't have detailed labelling, can I be sure it's safe?

Make sure all toys you buy are larger than your child's mouth to prevent choking (see page 27), and avoid small toys intended for older children. You could also avoid toys that make loud noises. Children have very sensitive ears and their hearing could be damaged. Ask to test the toy first.

Above all, check for sturdiness. All parts must be secured tightly, and avoid soft toys with loose buttons or other attachments.

Baby swings

Although it is by no means an essential piece of equipment, many parents discover that a mechanical swing can calm or entertain their baby when nothing else works. If you use one, don't put your baby in the seat until she can sit up on her own – usually not until she's six months or more.

- Only use a swing that stands firmly on the floor, and never use it for periods of more than 20 minutes at a time.
- Make sure that the base of the swing is wide and sturdy, and avoid using it on a hard surface such as concrete or ceramic tiles, in case it tips over.
- Always use the harness provided.

- Don't put your baby in the swing if there are older children running around nearby because they may bump into your baby or knock her over.
- Never leave your baby unattended in a swing.

Toys and playthings

Tough government regulations and rigorous testing by manufacturers mean that most children's toys on the market today are very safe. But, despite this, thousands of children still suffer toy-related injuries every year.

Although most injuries from toys consist of minor cuts or bruises, children can be seriously injured or even killed by dangerous toys.

MAKE BATHTIME FUN
Bath toys can help even the most reluctant bathers relax at bathtime. Plastic ducks are colourful favourites, but regularly check that squeakers have not come loose.

Toys suitable for your child's age

The important age recommendations printed on toy packaging reflect:

- the safety aspects of the toy and any possible choking hazards

- the physical ability of the child to play with the toy

- the ability of a child to understand how to use the toy

- the child's needs and interests at various levels of development.

But every child is different, and what is right for one child may not suit the skills or needs of another. Try to match the toy to your child's abilities. A toy that is too advanced for your child may be misused.

Newborn to one year
Choose brightly coloured, lightweight toys that appeal to your baby's senses.

- Cloth, plastic or board books.

- Large wooden or plastic blocks.

- Pots and pans.

- Rattles – check that these are at least 5cm (2in) across.

- Soft, washable toys, dolls or balls.

- Bright, moveable objects that your baby can see but are out of her reach.

- Floating bath toys.

- Squeezy toys – ensure that any squeakers cannot become detached.

One to three years
Toys should be sturdy to withstand your toddler's curious nature.

- Musical or spinning tops.

- Nesting blocks and stacking toys.

- Push and pull toys (with strings no longer than 20cm/8in).

- Toy telephones without cords.

Pre-school
Toys can be creative or imitate the activity of parents and older children.

- Blackboard and chalks.

- Building blocks.

- Non-toxic paints, crayons and clay.

- Housekeeping toys, such as tea sets.

- Outdoor toys, such as playhouses, slides and sandpits (with lids).

- Dressing-up clothes.

What should I look out for when buying my toddler a toy box?
While it's important to store your child's toys safely, toy boxes themselves can be hazardous. Large boxes with lids attached are particularly dangerous because your child can become trapped inside, and lids can fall on her head, body or fingers. For this reason, boxes without lids, or open plastic crates, are best. Often you can find styles that will stack neatly away.

If you do use a lidded toy box, choose one with sturdy supports that hold the lid open in any position, or, better still, a lightweight removable lid. If your toy box is large enough for your child to climb into and has a tight-fitting lid, make sure there are ventilation holes or a large gap between the lid and the box to prevent suffocation if your child becomes trapped inside.

THE IDEAL TOY BOX
This toy box is big enough to store all kinds of toys and yet your child can easily see and reach what's inside.

The following are some of the most common causes of accidents involving toys in the under-fives.

● **Toys with small parts** Small or broken parts can become lodged in your child's throat, nose or ear. Small parts or broken pieces are the cause of many injuries in children every year.

● **Broken toys** When a toy breaks, sharp or pointed edges may be exposed that can cause a serious injury. Something as innocent as a doll or a teddy bear may quickly become a hazard if your child pulls off an eye or removes a button, for example. Be especially careful with second-hand toys, which will have suffered more wear and tear.

● **Toys with loose strings and ribbons** These can easily become tangled around your baby or child's neck. Strings or cords on any children's toy should be no longer than 20cm (8in). Dangling objects, such as cot mobiles, can be particularly dangerous, so remove them as soon as your baby is able to pull herself up or by the age of five months, whichever comes first.

● **Wheeled toys** Injuries are caused not only when children fall off riding toys, but also when they ride them in the street with traffic or into ponds or pools. Use them only in secure areas, and ensure that the toy matches your child's physical abilities (see page 60).

● **Balloons** More children have suffocated or choked on uninflated or popped balloons than on any other type of toy. Because of their tendency to put everything in their mouths, children under three are most at risk, but inflated, uninflated or burst balloons should be kept away from children of all ages, especially the under-eights. Always pick up and discard broken pieces of balloon.

● **"Shooting" toys** Toys that shoot plastic objects are a common cause of eye injury. Never give a child a toy gun that fires anything (small water pistols may be an exception).

How can I ensure my child plays safely?

Playing with toys is an important part of your child's development. Choosing toys carefully and supervising your baby while she plays with them will assure that playtime is educational, fun and, most importantly, safe.

Supervise play at all times

★ Even when you have made your best efforts to choose the safest toys for your child, injuries can still occur.

★ Accidents happen most often when there is no adult supervision.

SUPERVISED PLAY
Even though older babies and children enjoy playing on their own, it's important to keep a close eye on them to be sure they are playing safely.

Store toys properly

★ Keep them off the floor, and encourage your child to pick up and put toys away. This will help keep her safe, as well as teach her to be responsible for her belongings.

★ Never store a toy in its original packaging. Staples can cause cuts and plastic wrapping can lead to choking or suffocation.

★ Throw away all packaging before giving the toy to your child.

Keep toys in good condition

★ Examine your child's playthings regularly to check for damaged or broken parts. Look for splinters on wooden toys, loose eyes or small parts on dolls, rips or exposed wires in stuffed toys, or signs of rust on metal toys.

★ Regularly wipe down your child's toys with a damp, soapy cloth and keep food away from them.

Teach your child to treat toys with respect

★ Even babies can be shown how to play with toys safely. Throwing toys, jumping on them or taking them apart can be dangerous.

" Since Matthew started walking, he's been **into everything**. I thought I'd **childproofed** all around the house but he keeps setting me new challenges! "

CRAIG is dad to 15-month-old Matthew

5

Safety in the home

Accidents in the home are the most common form of injury in children under four. Every year, thousands of children are admitted to hospital with injuries sustained from domestic mishaps. But being aware of the causes, and knowing which precautions to take to avoid danger, will significantly reduce the risks.

The first (and easiest) thing you can do to safeguard your child is simply to look around your home. Sit on the floor for a child's-eye view, and think about the things that are likely to attract his natural curiosity.

As your child grows, continue to see things from his perspective, and re-evaluate safety requirements. At the same time, teach him to become more aware of potential dangers, by explaining in simple terms when things can burn or hurt, for example.

Childproofing your home doesn't have to be complicated. Simply removing sharp items from your kitchen's floor-level cupboards, fitting safety locks and electrical socket covers or securing any unsteady furniture means you are childproofing (see pages 44–45). Whatever measures you take, they should help make you – and your child – feel safer and more relaxed.

Fire safety

House fires are the biggest single cause of accidental death of children in the home, mostly as a result of smoke inhalation. Following recommended safety rules will significantly reduce the risk of this happening to you – and save lives.

- Fit smoke alarms (see right).
- Don't smoke in your house. If you must, ensure cigarettes and matches are extinguished completely, and dispose of them safely. Keep matches and lighters out of your child's reach.
- Work out an escape plan for you and your family. Get advice from your local fire brigade.
- As soon as your child is old enough, tell him what to do if he discovers a fire or hears the alarm.
- Keep all doors shut at night.
- Keep a fire extinguisher in your kitchen. A fire blanket is handy, too.
- Repair old or worn electrical flexes and do not overload electrical sockets.

Smoke alarms

If you don't already have a smoke alarm, now is the time to invest in one. Many alarms are battery-operated (some have 10-year batteries), while others can be wired to the mains or attached to light fittings. All of them do the same job – they can give you vital extra time to get out of your house in the event of fire.

- When buying a smoke alarm look for a Kitemark and/or British Standard Number BS 5446.
- Test the alarm regularly – once a month is recommended – and replace the battery once a year.
- Always have a smoke alarm installed just outside your kitchen, and at least one on every floor of your house.
- A carbon monoxide monitor is also recommended if you have a gas cooker or gas central heating. This alerts you to the presence of carbon monoxide, an odourless gas that can be lethal.

Dealing with burns and scalds

Between the ages of six months and two years, your child is more likely to burn or scald himself than at any other time in his life. Acting fast can make a burn much less serious than it might be otherwise.

What to do

• No matter how small or large the burn, immediately flood the affected area with cold running water for at least 10 minutes. Keep the rest of your child's body warm.

• If clothes are not stuck to your child's skin around the burned area, remove them (cut them, if need be) but if anything is sticking to the burn, do not attempt to remove it.

• If the burn is large, severe or you are at all concerned, call 999.

• Cover the area with a sterile dressing or any non-fluffy material to keep out infection. Cling wrap can make a good temporary covering if nothing else is available. Never apply creams or lotions to the skin.

• Large burns should always be seen by a doctor, but even smaller

SOOTHING TREATMENT
Take some of the heat out of a burn by immediately holding it under cold running water for about 10 minutes.

burns may need medical attention, especially if the skin blisters. Don't break blisters, as this can cause infection.

• If your child's clothes catch fire, drop him to the floor and roll him in a coat, blanket or rug. Don't try to remove his

clothes. Follow the first aid advice above and call 999. If the burn is electrical, switch off electricity at the mains before applying first aid.

• Hold chemical burns under cold water for 20 minutes and call 999.

• If a fire starts in your home, shut the door on it, leave the building, and call the fire brigade immediately.

Fireplaces and heaters

Any fire with an open flame should have a protective fireguard around it. Ideally, it should be fixed to the wall.

• Never leave your child unattended in a room with a burning open fire, even if it has a fireguard.

• Don't place anything on the guard.

• Keep all furniture at least 1m (3ft) away from an open fire.

• Never let your child see you throwing things onto the fire.

• Keep temperatures down on radiators to avoid burns, and teach your child that they are hot and must never be touched.

• If you use electric heaters, keep your child, and any furniture, well away from them. Never place a heater on any surface but the floor.

Kitchen safety

For a small child, the kitchen is the most dangerous place in the house. Ideally, you should keep your baby or child out of the kitchen at all times, but often this isn't practical. Aim at least to keep him out when you are cooking. Installing a stair gate at your kitchen door will help.

Cupboards and drawers

● Use safety catches to keep cupboards, drawers and doors off-limits to your child.

● Store cleaners, bleach, furniture polish, dishwasher soap and other dangerous products in a high cabinet, preferably lockable, out of sight. These substances are lethal and should never be left within reach.

● If you have no option but to store some items under the sink, buy safety locks that refasten automatically every time you close the cupboard.

● Never transfer toxic substances into containers that look as though they might hold food or drink.

● Keep knives, forks, scissors and other sharp instruments separate from safer kitchen utensils, and in a latched drawer.

● Store plastic bags in a drawer or cabinet with a safety catch.

OUT OF HARM'S WAY
The most effective way to protect your child from burns and scalds when you're cooking – and, most likely, distracted – is to keep her out of the kitchen.

Expert tips

The cooker is potentially the most dangerous kitchen appliance.

● Always turn pot handles towards the back of the stove.

● Whenever you're cooking or carrying hot food, keep your child out of the kitchen so you don't trip over him – a stair gate across the kitchen doorway is a good idea.

● When cooking, try to use the back burners only.

● If you have a gas stove, turn the dials firmly to the "off" position, and, if they're easy to remove, do so when you are not cooking.

● Install a cooker or oven guard.

● Teach your child that the oven is hot and not for touching, and keep reinforcing this message.

Aluminium foil and cling-wrap boxes can also be hazardous, as their serrated edges can cut little fingers.

- Unplug appliances on work counters when not in use, and keep cords out of your child's reach.

Household appliances

Fridges, freezers, washing machines and tumble driers could prove fatal if your child becomes trapped in one by climbing inside. If the door closes on them, tight-fitting seals will cut off the air supply, and a child's cries may go unheard. Warn your child of the dangers of playing inside an appliance, and keep all doors firmly closed after use. When discarding appliances, remove the doors first. There are safety factors worth noting with other household appliances.

Rubbish bins

These can make unwitting playgrounds. Young children enjoy nothing more than rooting around in search of interesting playthings.

- Keep your bin locked in a cupboard, if possible.

- When disposing of broken glass, always wrap it well in newspaper before placing it in the bin.

- Tie knots in plastic bags before throwing them away.

CUPBOARD LOCKS
Some safety locks fit inside a cupboard door, allowing you to open the door a little way before releasing the catch. These catches automatically lock themselves as you close the door.

- Keep your microwave switched off at the mains when it's not in use.
- Never use the microwave to warm baby bottles or food, as it heats things unevenly, leaving pockets hot enough to scald your child's mouth.
- When loading the dishwasher, always place cutlery in the appropriate tray, handle-side up, so that no sharp points or edges face upwards when the door is open.
- Always make sure that your dishwasher door is securely closed, unless you are loading or unloading the dishes. When the door is open, keep your child out of the way. As well as being a dangerous tripping hazard, he may be tempted to stand or sit on the open door, and an unanchored machine may tip over.

Stair gates

Once your child starts to crawl and preferably beforehand – it's best to install stair gates at the top and bottom of your stairway.

● There are many types of stair gates on the market; if you are choosing one for the top of a stairway, make sure that it screws into the wall for extra strength. Stair gates that use pressure or suction are not recommended for use at the top of the stairs, as your child could push through them and fall. Accordion-style gates, which can trap arms or even necks, are also not recommended.

● Make sure the gap between any stair gate and the floor is less than 5cm (2in) wide.

● Leave the first two or three stairs at the bottom of your stairway free, so that your baby can practise climbing on them.

Windows

Falls make up a large proportion of injuries in children under five. The majority of these are from windows, furniture, stairs and playground equipment.

For this reason, avoid putting any furniture under windows, where it will tempt little climbers, and make sure there are catches or locks on all frames. This will go a long way to giving you peace of mind, but do make sure that all windows can be opened quickly by you, in case of a fire. Keep keys nearby but out of your child's reach – you could even tape them to the upper frame.

The majority of falls from windows happen during spring and summer, because they are more likely to be left open. If you need to open your windows, do so from the top rather than the bottom. If this is not possible, install safety bars or screens on the lower halves of windows that only an adult or older child can push out from the inside in an emergency.

Be sure to tie up all curtain and blind cords around wall brackets to keep them out of reach; cords with loops should be cut to prevent your child from strangling himself.

Staying safe on the stairs

Around 60,000 children under the age of five are injured falling down stairs every year.

● As soon as your child is able to climb up and downstairs, spend time with him teaching him how to do so safely. Young children (under the age of two and a half) might find it easier to crawl upstairs rather than walk, and climb downstairs backwards, as if coming down a ladder.

● Never let your child climb up or downstairs unsupervised until you are absolutely sure of his competence.

● Make sure your banisters are sturdy, with less than 10cm (4in) between the posts. If the gaps are any larger than that, your baby or child could get his neck or head caught. Banisters with large gaps between them may need boarding up.

● Banisters should have no horizontal bars or slats – your child

Questions & Answers

How can I reduce the risk of my child getting an electric shock?
The most effective step you can take is to install plastic socket covers on all sockets that are not being used. It's also a good idea to get into the habit of unplugging appliances when not in use, and using socket covers.

Children may be tempted to chew on power cables, as well as tug them, and this can also be a cause of electrocution. Use cord shorteners to tidy up loose wires, and make sure cable is always held in place behind heavy furniture. Alternatively, staple or tape it to the floor or walls.

Check electric cable frequently and replace any worn cable. Never run cables or flexes under carpets or rugs.

Expert tips

A well-stocked medicine and first aid cabinet is essential, but it must be locked and kept out of reach of children.

• Keep all medications locked away, and ensure that their containers are shatterproof and have safety caps.

• When a course of prescribed medication is finished, don't keep any that's left over. Flush it away.

• Never tell your child that medicine tastes good or that it's "like sweeties".

• Store vitamins in a safe place, too, as children can overdose on them.

• If your child does swallow medicine, or any poison of any kind, get whatever you can out of his mouth and **call 999 immediately**. Have the bottle in your hand so that you can tell the emergency operator what was ingested and roughly how much. Do not give your child anything to eat or drink unless the emergency operator tells you to do so.

THE BATHROOM CABINET
Your bathroom cabinet or first aid cupboard should be positioned well out of reach of your child. Medicines and other dangerous items should be kept locked away.

may use them as a ladder. If need be, remove them or board them up.
• Keep stairs clutter-free. If you are in the habit of leaving things on the stairs ready to take on the next trip, place a sturdy box in the hallway instead to accommodate these items.
• Leave a night light on in the hallway for older children needing to get up in the night.

Bathroom safety

The simplest way to avoid bathroom injuries is to make this room inaccessible unless your child is with an adult. This may mean installing a latch or lock on the outside of the door at adult height.

A child can drown in as little as 5cm (2in) of water, so it is not only the bath that poses a threat: toilet bowls, nappy buckets and sinks, for example, can be just as dangerous. There are other potential hazards to try to avoid as well.
• Keep toothpaste, mouthwashes, soaps and shampoos high up or in a cabinet with a safety latch or locks. Sharp objects, such as razor blades, scissors and nail clippers should also be locked away.

NON–SLIP BATH
A non-slip bath mat or adhesive strips will protect your child from nasty bumps when he's in the bath.

Water temperature

Injuries caused by scalding bath water often involve large parts of the body. This is why it is important that you run the cold water into the bath before adding the hot water, and always test the temperature before letting your child get in. A child exposed to a very hot tap could sustain a third-degree burn, which requires hospitalization and skin grafts.

One of the most effective ways to prevent burns and scalds is to turn your hot-water thermostat down. Safety experts recommend that hot water should come out of your taps at no more than 45°C (113°F).

• Remove all electrical items, such as hairdryers, razors and radios, from the bathroom.

• Never throw used razor blades, toothbrushes or other potentially dangerous materials into the bathroom wastebasket.

• Check that shower doors or other surfaces are made of safety glass or shatterproof material.

• Throw away soap when it is small enough to fit inside your child's mouth. Children can choke on soap.

• Many accidents occur while a carer leaves a baby or toddler unattended "just for a minute" to answer the telephone. Take your child with you, invest in a cordless telephone or switch on the answering machine.

In the bath

Never, *under any circumstances*, leave your baby or child unsupervised in the bath. Children can drown in seconds. If you have to go to the door or phone, take your child out of the bath, wrap him in a towel and take him with you when you go to answer it. Or, ignore it!

Remember that bath seats and rings designed for young babies are meant to be bathing aids, not safety aids. They will not stop your child drowning if he is left unattended.

There are other important bathtime safety considerations.

• Place a non-slip mat or strips on the bottom of your bath.

• Always run the cold water before the hot, and then mix the water so

that it feels just warm. Test it with your inner wrist or elbow before putting your baby in the water.

• Always use both hands to lift your baby into and out of the bath.

• Cover taps with soft flannels during bathtime.

Toilets

• Get into the habit of keeping the toilet lid down at all times – fix on a toilet lock if you want to be particularly careful.

• Never leave toilet cleaner in the toilet bowl to soak. Wash it and flush it away.

What safety equipment should I have?

As well as the larger safety items you will need, such as stair gates, there are many smaller, ingenious safety devices, all designed to help you childproof your home. Anything with sharp edges, hinges or drawers could cause injury to your baby or child, so look around each room from his viewpoint to spot the dangers.

★ **Guard against falling furniture** One of the most common injuries caused by a piece of furniture happens when it falls on top of a baby or child. Bookshelves, chests of drawers, television trolleys and tables are particularly lethal, as they may become attractive climbing equipment for your child, who may then pull them over. Secure freestanding bookshelves, cabinets or any other furniture which is unstable with L–brackets screwed to the wall if necessary (available from hardware stores) and make sure all your large and heavy furniture is resting solidly on the floor, with no wobbly legs.

★ **Protect your child from nasty knocks** Check all around your home for any hard edges or sharp corners that could injure him if he fell or bumped his head against them. Coffee tables are a particular hazard – if possible, don't keep furniture like this in the middle of the room where it is easy to knock,

especially if you have a child who is learning to walk or an energetic toddler who likes to run around. Another potential hazard is the use of tablecloths, particularly on higher tables. If tugged by your baby or child, these could bring down crockery and cutlery, and perhaps even scalding liquids, such as hot drinks or soup, with disastrous

COVER SHARP EDGES
Furniture with sharp corners can be made safe for your baby or child by simply adding padded corner protectors. These slot on easily and will help prevent nasty bumps or bruises.

consequences. It is safer to stop using them altogether while your baby or child is so young.

★ **Be aware of the risks from glass** Glass or mirrored panels, such as on cabinets or tables, should be kept out of bounds if at all possible, but if not, should be fitted with shatterproof glass. A less expensive alternative worth considering is to affix safety film to these surfaces. This invisible film stops glass from shattering over your child if it breaks.

★ **Secure the television** Make sure that any television set – no matter what size it is – is placed on a firm and stable piece of furniture, which preferably is low. Push it back against the wall, discourage your child from playing with the television controls, especially around the back of

the set, and install a guard to protect fingers from getting trapped in VCR or DVD slots.

★ **Check old furniture and walls for lead–based paint** This is highly toxic, and you can buy testing kits for this purpose from hardware shops. If stripping furniture, do it outside – avoid stripping paint in the home, as this can release poisonous lead dust into the air.

★ **Safeguard doors and drawers** Foam stoppers on doors prevent them from slamming on little hands or fingers. Safety catches on cupboards and drawers keep their contents out of bounds. They also prevent trapped fingers and guard against drawers being pulled completely out. Dangerous or unsuitable items should always be stored and locked away out of reach.

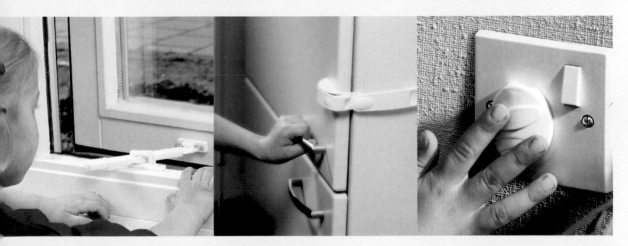

MAKE WINDOWS SAFE
Fitting safety catches to high windows that restrict the width of an open window will prevent your child falling, while still allowing for ventilation. Choose a design that an adult will be able to release quickly in an emergency. Low windows should be boarded, made of toughened glass or covered with safety film.

GUARD YOUR FRIDGE
As well as preventing your hungry toddler from raiding your fridge and making a mess, a fridge lock will protect him from heavy bottles or jars that may fall off the high shelves or from the fridge toppling over on top of him as he struggles to reach up for something.

AVOID ELECTROCUTION
Socket covers are easy to fit and should be used throughout your home. They will stop your baby or child inserting his fingers and other objects in the sockets, and so avoid electrocution. Always unplug electrical items when not in use and remember to put back the socket cover.

" Our garden's not very big, but it's perfect for Kim to **run about** in. We're going to buy a climbing frame when he's a bit older. Perhaps it will help him **burn off** some of that energy! "

LIZZIE is mum to two-year-old Kim

6

Garden safety

Your baby or child will love being outside, but the best way to keep her safe is to stay with her at all times. A garden may present a whole array of potential hazards of which you need to be fully aware, but this doesn't mean you can't make it a safe and pleasurable environment in which to play.

Garden gates and fences

The most basic safety check you can carry out is to ensure that your garden is secure so that your child can't get out (and no one else can get in) without you knowing about it. Check that all gates fasten securely, and replace latches, locks and hinges as necessary. Locks should be high enough to prevent your child reaching them.

If your gate or fence has horizontal bars that could be climbed on, remove them or board them up. A child can wriggle through the smallest space in a broken fence or hedge, so make sure that there are no holes in fences or gates. Also, look for exposed nails or loose boards and mend them immediately.

A safe environment

Once you are satisfied that your boundaries are secure, look around the rest of the garden.

● Check paving stones for cracks, which your child could trip over, or moss, which can be very slippery when wet.

● If you have a washing line or rotary drier, ensure the lines are kept high up to prevent the risk of strangulation.

● Don't leave hosepipes or other gardening equipment lying around (see page 49).

● Keep your child well away from barbecues and bonfires, which stay hot for a long time after you have finished with them.

● If you have a greenhouse, think about taking it down, or cover the lower panes of glass with safety film or boards.

● Don't let your baby or child play in the soil, as there is a risk of infection from animal faeces (see page 52). If she does do some digging, wash her hands and face thoroughly straight away.

Questions & Answers

How can I make my balcony safe for my child?
Never leave your child unsupervised on a balcony or deck at any time, and make sure the door leading to it is kept locked when it's not in use. If your balcony railings have horizontal or vertical openings wider than 10cm (4in), you need to make some modifications.

If the spindles are vertical, consider adding to them to make the openings smaller. Alternatively, you could cover your railings with garden fencing, boarding or cloth. Secure these materials to the railings with screws or plastic cord ties (avoid staples, as they can cut your child's hands and are a serious choking hazard).

Covering the railings is particularly important if the spindles run horizontally, as this will stop your child from being able to climb. Keep furniture off your balcony, as this may also encourage your child to climb.

Water safety

Drowning in garden ponds or pools is one of the largest causes of domestic accidents for under-fives. Babies and young children can drown in a couple of centimetres of water.

Never leave your child unattended near any kind of water, whether it's a paddling pool or a filled bucket. Even containers, such as bins, troughs or old paint tins, which have collected rain water can be lethal. Do not leave these lying around where your child can reach them, and if you have a water butt or any other large water vessel in your garden, seal it safely to stop over-curious climbers.

If you have a paddling pool, make sure that you empty it as soon as your child has finished playing in it. Once it is emptied, the safest options are either to deflate it or leave it turned upside down.

"Guy is a real water baby and can't wait to get in the paddling pool on warm days. It's great watching him having fun."

GILL is mum to three-year-old Guy

Garden ponds

The safest thing you can do with a garden pond or water feature is to fill it in. Some parents choose to fill a pond temporarily with sand until their child is older.

If you decide to retain your pond, you will need to cover it using rigid, heavy-duty steel mesh, which should be placed well above the surface of the pond. Mesh that is on or below the surface won't prevent drowning. Fencing materials, such as chicken wire, are unsuitable, as they will sag when any weight is on them.

The mesh needs to be very secure, and the frame must be solid. Make sure your child can't crawl beneath the wire or pull it to one side.

If you decide to fence your pond off, make sure the fencing cannot be climbed by young children. A vertical-railed fence is best, with bars no more than 10cm (4in) apart, and no less than 1.2m (3ft 6in) in height. Any gates should meet similar specifications and be kept locked.

Be especially vigilant in other people's gardens. Eighty per cent of drownings happen in the garden of a friend, relative or neighbour. If your neighbours have ponds in their gardens, ask them to check their sides of fences or boundaries for any gaps you may have missed which your child could get through.

TOOL SHEDS
Store garden tools and toxic substances securely in the shed. Keep it locked and make sure the key is put away out of your child's reach.

Poisonous plants

Every year, thousands of children are poisoned by touching or eating plants, so it's a good idea to find out exactly which plants, shrubs and trees are growing in your garden and remove or secure any that are harmful. Be particularly wary of berries and fungi. Babies and young children will eat flowers, berries, bulbs or anything else that catches their eye,

so before you buy a new plant, check whether it is poisonous.

A reputable garden nursery will be able to identify any plants or trees in your garden that you are unsure of. Take along a cutting, including a good length of stem, leaves and any flowers or berries it produces. Many harmless-looking plants in your garden can cause skin irritation when they are touched, or sickness

Expert tips

Garden sheds, garages or basements must be kept locked and off-limits to your child.

- Weedkillers, paints, varnishes, pesticides or any other toxic substances should be locked away. Never store a substance in anything other than its own container.

- Keep all tools or any item that could be remotely dangerous locked up and well out of reach.

- If you have an automatic garage door opener, make sure your child is nowhere near before you operate it.

- If you are using chemicals or outdoor power equipment, keep your child indoors under someone else's watchful eye. Turn off electricals if your child comes near. Never let her ride on machinery, such as lawnmowers, even if you are supervising, and switch off and unplug electrical tools if you are not using them.

if they are ingested. Other plants can be poisonous, even fatal, if leaves, flowers, berries or bulbs are eaten.

As your child grows, teach him never to pick and eat anything from a plant, no matter how good it looks, without asking you. It is especially important to reinforce this safety warning if you have a vegetable garden with edible produce.

If you suspect that your child may have eaten a poisonous plant:

- remove any remaining parts of the plant from his mouth
- ring your doctor or your local Accident and Emergency department for advice on what to do next
- do not make your child vomit

Checklist

Poisonous garden plants include:

- alder
- bryony
- cherry laurel
- deadly nightshade (its shiny purple berries may be very tempting)
- foxglove
- ivy with berries
- monkshood
- woody nightshade
- yew.

Plants that can cause sickness include:

- bluebells (root bulbs)
- daffodils (bulbs)
- delphinium
- fuchsia
- holly (berries and leaves)
- honeysuckle (berries)
- laburnum (seeds and pods)
- lily of the valley
- lupin
- mistletoe
- potato plant (except the potato itself)
- privet
- pyracantha (berries)
- rhododendron
- rhubarb (leaves, and flesh when raw)
- snowdrops
- wisteria.

KNOW YOUR PLANTS
Familiarize yourself with the plants in your garden, so that you know which are safe to keep, and which to dig up.

- keep a sample of the plant and take it with you in a plastic bag if you need to see a doctor.

Play areas

Although you should always ensure that your entire garden is as hazard-free as possible, you may want to create a special safe area in your garden just for your baby or child, perhaps with play equipment, such as a slide, swing or playhouse. This area should be laid out well away from flowerbeds or other soily areas, with plenty of space for running around.

If you do decide to have play equipment, the ground area beneath it and around it needs to be soft. Never install play equipment on concrete – choose grass or lay a soft substance, such as loose woodchips, rubber or sand, in order to cushion any inevitable falls.

Loose, soft materials should ideally be laid down to a minimum depth of 23cm (9in) and should extend to at least 1.8m (72in) in all directions around stationary equipment.

This surface will need regular maintenance to keep it at a safe depth at all times. Also, if your child is very young, you will need to make sure that she doesn't put woodchip or any soft material you have used on the play area base in her mouth.

OUTDOOR PLAY EQUIPMENT
Always follow the manufacturer's instructions when assembling outdoor play equipment, and regularly check it for signs of wear and tear.

Garden toys

All outdoor toys you choose for your child should be:
- suitable for your child's age
- weatherproof and not warp or deteriorate if left outside

- properly assembled following the manufacturer's instructions (check regularly that no screws or fittings have worked loose).

When installing play equipment:
- fix it securely to the ground so

Reptiles and birds

- Over the past few years there has been an increase in the popularity of exotic pets, such as lizards, snakes and turtles. This has triggered major government health warnings, because nine out of ten reptiles are thought to carry salmonella, which can be fatal in humans and is a particular threat to children under five, as well as pregnant women. Even indirect contact can be dangerous. Do not keep reptiles as pets.

- A disease known as psittacosis is a risk for anyone who keeps a bird as a pet. Particles from droppings can be inhaled and transmit an infection which can cause a strain of pneumonia, requiring treatment with powerful antibiotics. Close contact with caged birds is also known to increase the risk of lung cancer in later life. Your child should never share a room with a caged bird; birds should be kept outdoors, if possible.

that it can't work loose, and follow the manufacturer's instructions

- ensure there are no sharp points, nuts or bolts sticking out
- make sure that ladders, slides, platforms and bridgeways have guard rails to prevent falls
- make regular checks of your child's play area, and replace any broken or worn-out components.

Pet safety

Having a pet has many benefits for your family, but hygiene will need to be your number-one priority if you have a baby or young child. All animals can carry infections, and some of these can be dangerous if passed on to humans. To keep your family safe, there are a few simple safety guidelines to follow.

- Keep household pets well away from all areas where food is prepared or cooked.
- Never let your pet defecate in your garden or any area where your child plays. Regularly check for faeces and clear it up straight away if you find any.
- If you have a sandpit, always keep it well covered when it's not in use. This will prevent any animals using it as a toilet, and keep it dry for the next time your child wants to play in it.

Toxoplasmosis

Cats and dogs can spread a number of diseases. Toxoplasmosis, for example, is an infection transmitted by cat faeces and has symptoms similar to glandular fever. It can also be transmitted via raw meat.

This disease is of greatest risk to pregnant women, as it can cause fetal deformities, including brain and eye damage. Young babies and children, or anyone with a weakened immune system, are also more at risk of serious side-effects.

- Always wash your child's hands if she's been playing in the garden or handling a pet.
- Discourage your child from eating snacks while playing outdoors, and remember to wash her hands before eating.
- If you are pregnant, always wear gloves when clearing away cat faeces or handling your cat's litter tray – or, better still, ask someone else to do it.

Toxocariasis

Dogs, and sometimes cats, carry toxocariasis. This is a worm infection in their intestines that can be passed on to humans. Almost all puppies are born with it. Eggs are excreted in faeces and become infectious around two weeks later. They can survive for two years or more. Children playing in parks or gardens can pick up their sticky eggs on their hands and are infected when they put their hands in their mouths. Symptoms include mild fever, stomach ache and, in some cases, serious eye damage.

To protect your child:
- worm your dog or cat regularly – consult your vet for advice
- scoop up faeces in a plastic bag and dispose of it carefully; always wash your hands afterwards

" Poppy loves cuddling her pet rabbit, and really enjoys helping to feed and care for him. She's even started to remember now that she has to wash her hands when she has finished stroking him. "

SARAH is mum to three-year-old
Poppy

• consult your doctor if you suspect that your child has been exposed to toxocariasis, or if she is showing any worrying symptoms.

Cat scratches

A bite or scratch from a cat may cause a rare illness known as cat-scratch fever, in which a lymph node near the scratch swells, and a blister may appear near the site of the scratch. Children may also have a fever, a rash and a headache.

If your child has been bitten or scratched by a cat, clean the wound carefully with antiseptic, and see your doctor if your child has any of the symptoms of cat-scratch fever.

Farm animals

Children can also pick up infections from farms. Cryptosporidium passes from infected animals to children who touch them. It causes diarrhoea that can last for a week. An infected child can pass the infection on to others. Children should always wash their hands after playing with farm animals.

" While Iona's still young, I prefer taking her out in **her sling** than in her pushchair. It gives me more freedom and she feels secure and seems to love the **closeness**. "

ANNIE is mum to five-month-old Iona

7

Out & about

Trips out and about with your baby or child are an important part of the daily routine, but once you're away from the security of your home environment, you need to be extra careful. Whether you are driving him in the car, pushing him in a buggy or simply walking along together, you will want to keep him safe at all times.

Every year, more children are killed in road accidents than by any other cause. Many of these deaths could be prevented if proper car seat restraints were used.

The single most important thing you can do to keep your child safe in the car is to buy, install and use an approved car seat for every journey (see below and pages 56–57). This is vital – even on the shortest trips: most fatal crashes happen at speeds of less than 25 miles per hour, and within five miles of home.

Buying a car seat

Take your time when buying any car seat for your child.

● Not every seat will fit properly in every car. Try the seat before you buy it, and make sure it can be fitted into the back seat of your car, exactly to the manufacturer's instructions.

● It is very important that the seat is secure. If it wobbles in any direction, it is either wrongly fitted or not suitable for your make of car. Some retailers have experts who can check the fit for you.

● Keep the car seat instructions and refer to them regularly to ensure that the seat is always safe.

● If you have two cars, or if your baby regularly travels in someone else's car, make sure the seat you choose fits both.

● Choose a car seat according to your baby or child's weight, not his age. As soon as he reaches the weight limit for one seat, it's time to buy a bigger seat (see pages 56–57).

● Don't be tempted to buy a second-hand car seat, as it could have been involved in an accident or have been dropped. Even if the seat looks perfect, it could have damage you would be unable to detect.

● For the same reason, it's advisable to buy a new car seat if you have been involved in a crash.

(see below and pages 56–57)

Expert tips

Follow these tips for safe car travel.

● Never leave your baby or child unattended in a car.

● Always use child locks on passenger doors. Check they are on when travelling in other people's cars.

● Consider attaching a small mirror to your passenger visor so that you can keep an eye on your child.

● Never keep anything dangerous within reach of your child (including bags of shopping) in case he throws something while you are driving.

● Never travel with your baby on your lap – always use a suitable car seat.

● Make sure that luggage or other heavy items are stowed safely.

● When operating electric windows or sun roofs, and when slamming car doors shut, always check first that your baby or child is not in the way.

Which type of car seat should I choose?

As you should never compromise your child's safety while on the road, a car seat is probably the most important piece of equipment you will buy for him. There are several types to choose from, suitable for various stages of your child's development, from newborn right through until he's tall enough to use an adult seat belt safely.

Infant carriers

★ Infant carriers are suitable for newborn babies up until they reach 10kg (22lb) or 13kg (29lb) in weight, depending on the design of the car seat.

★ They are only used in a rear-facing position, which is by far the safest position for newborn babies. In fact, the longer you can keep your baby in a rear-facing seat, the better in terms of his safety while travelling in the car.

★ A rear-facing car seat should never be placed in the front passenger seat of the car where there is an airbag fitted. Airbags have been responsible for serious injuries and even death in a number of young children. The centre seat in the back is the safest place for your baby or child to travel. If you must place your child's car seat in the front seat of a car with an airbag, deactivate the airbag first, then reactivate it when you remove the car seat.

★ Infant seats have a five-point safety harness and are secured using the adult seat belt. Adjust the five-point harness to suit the thickness of your baby's clothes on every trip. You should be able to slide only two fingers between the strap and your child's chest.

Rear- and forward-facing seats

★ These are also called infant-toddler seats. They are suitable from birth in the rear-facing position, and then from around 9kg (20lb) can be turned round and used facing forwards, until your child reaches 18kg (40lb). They have their own five-point harness and are secured using the adult seat belt.

AN INFANT CARRIER
Used in a rear-facing position, preferably in the centre back seat of your car, this is the safest way for your young baby to travel in the car.

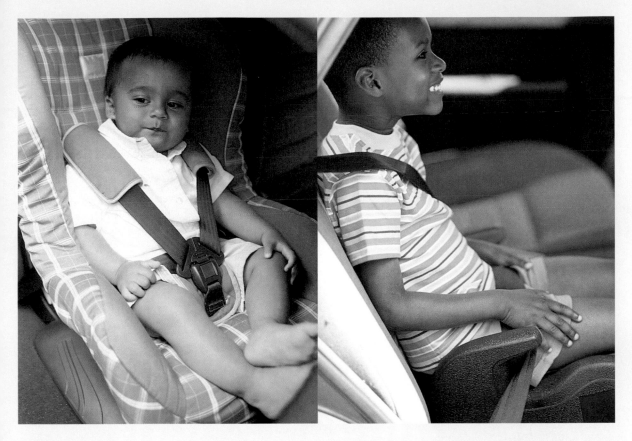

A FORWARD–FACING SEAT
Suitable from 9kg (20lb), this seat follows on from an infant carrier.
Some, like this one, have a five-point harness and can be reclined;
others use the car seat belt to secure both your child and the seat.

A BOOSTER SEAT
A booster seat will raise your older child to a level that ensures he
can sit securely using the adult seat belt. Because he can see out of
the window, a booster seat can also help to ease travel sickness.

Forward–facing seats

★ If you decide to buy an infant carrier to begin with – and this is the recommended option for the first few months – you will need a new seat when your child reaches a weight of 10kg or 13kg (22lb or 29lb) or more (depending on the weight limit of your infant car seat). Forward-facing seats are suitable for babies weighing at least 9kg (20lb) and last until your child is 18kg or 25kg (40lb or 55lb), again depending on the model.

★ Some forward-facing seats don't have a separate five-point harness, but instead use the adult seat belt to secure both the seat and your child.

Booster seats

★ Once your child reaches around 18kg (40lb), he will progress to a booster seat. This should always be used with an adaptor that positions the car safety belt to fit your child properly – the lap belt should be tight and low across your child's hips and the shoulder belt should lie flat across his shoulder, away from his neck and face.

Checklist

Here's how to avoid accidents in your pushchair.

- Don't overload the pushchair – in particular, avoid hanging bags on the handles, as this can cause it to tip up.

- Take care when crossing the road. Never push the pushchair off the kerb until you are absolutely sure there is no oncoming traffic.

- Use reflective stickers to help make your pushchair more visible at night or in poor weather.

- Never leave your baby or child unattended in his pushchair.

Choosing a pushchair

A pushchair is one of the most important pieces of equipment you will need during the first few years of your child's life.

There are a number of different types to choose from.

- **Two-in-one pushchairs** These can be used as a pram or a pushchair. The carriage position allows a newborn to ride almost flat on his back, usually in a rear-facing or forward-facing position, while the stroller position lets your older baby ride sitting upright or in a reclining position. Three-in-one models come with a separate carrycot that attaches to the chassis for use during the first few weeks.

- **Lightweight buggies** These fold up neatly, and are easy to carry, but they're not as comfortable or adjustable as larger models and, because they do not fully recline, they are suitable only for babies from the age of six months.

- **Travel systems** These are like the two-in-one or three-in-one models but they also support infant car seats, and can be used until toddlerhood.

- **Multiple-occupancy pushchairs** These allow parents to push two or more children at once. Tandem models generally manoeuvre more easily and fold up more compactly.

- **Jogging or all-terrain pushchairs (ATPs)** ATPs feature three large bicycle-style wheels mounted to a lightweight frame. Some models are unsuitable for newborns because they do not offer a fully reclining position.

A safe ride

Whatever type of pushchair you choose, bear in mind the following questions, and ask advice from retailers, if necessary.

- **Does it reach the required safety standards?** Look for BS 7409.

- **Does it have a fully reclining position?** Your newborn should be carried flat for the first few months, but not all pushchairs and buggies can be adjusted to this position.

- **Does it have a five-point harness?** All new pushchairs do now come with these, but if you are buying a second-hand pushchair you may need to buy a harness separately. If so, look for BS 6684.

- **Are the brakes in good working order?** Test them with the weight of your baby in the pushchair, on a slope as well as on a flat surface. Check your brakes and the overall condition of your pushchair every few months.

- **Does it have a safety locking device?** This will prevent it from collapsing or folding up when your baby is in it. But you need to

Out with a toddler

Keep your toddler in his pushchair when you are walking out in busy streets. It's best not to let him walk until you can leave crowded areas for somewhere more child-friendly, such as a park or playground.

If you need a change from the pushchair, try using some reins that fit like a harness. Although these don't suit everyone, some parents find them invaluable, as they enable your child to have a little independence without compromising his safety. Wrist straps are not recommended, however, as they could easily become tangled.

RIDING HIGH
Back packs can give you both a great sense of freedom. To be safe and comfortable, they need to be sturdy, padded and used with a harness.

ensure that your child cannot release the mechanism.
● Are there spaces where fingers could get caught? Give it a thorough check all over.

Baby carriers

The safest way to carry a new baby around is in a sling, and these are perfect for the first few months. When your baby can sit unsupported, you may prefer a back pack.
● Take your baby with you when you shop for a back pack, so that you can try it out. Make sure the back pack supports his back, and that leg holes are small enough to prevent him slipping through.
● When choosing a sling or back pack, look for sturdy material and comfort. If you buy a back pack, make sure the aluminium frame is padded, so that your baby won't be hurt if he bumps against it.
● When you are wearing a back pack or sling, be sure to bend at the knees, not the waist, if you need to pick something up. Otherwise, your baby may slip out of the carrier.
● Babies over five months may become restless in a back pack, so be sure the harness is always used. A restless baby may brace his feet on the frame, changing his weight distribution. You should always make sure your child is seated properly before you start to move.

Questions & Answers

Is it safe to carry my child on the back of my bike?

Only children over the age of one, who can sit well unsupported, should be carried on an adult's bike. To make sure it is safe:

• a rear-mounted seat should be securely attached over the back wheel and have spoke guards to prevent feet and hands from being caught in the wheels

• it should have a high back and a sturdy shoulder harness and lap belt that will support a sleeping child

• a lightweight bike helmet must always be worn.

• Most accidents involving slings or back packs happen when parents fall over. Make sure you are wearing suitable shoes and take care in slippery conditions.

Bikes and trikes

Wheeled toys, such as scooters, bicycles and tricycles, are fun, but they have their own safety hazards.

• Don't give your child a wheeled toy until you are sure he is physically able to handle it. For a first bike, choose a tricycle that's built low to the ground with big wheels.

• Bikes and trikes should only be used in protected places. Don't allow your child to ride on the street, near

GOING FOR A RIDE
The garden and a park with plenty of open space are safe places for your young child to practise her cycling skills.

traffic or swimming pools or ponds.

• Always put a helmet on your child when he's riding a bike or scooter.

Staying safe on the roads and in public places

Child development experts say that from the age of three, your child is old enough to begin learning road safety. From this age, and even before, you can teach your child to stay on the pavement and that roads are extremely dangerous. Discuss:

• how you should cross the road

• that it's important to look and listen

• that you should use pedestrian crossings wherever possible – and always practise what you preach.

At the shops

• Keep your child with you at all times when you are out – never

leave her unattended in her pushchair, even if it's just to "pop in" to a shop.

• Teach your older child what to do if she gets separated from you. Point out shop assistants and stress that she should never leave the shop.

Stranger danger

• Teach your child to raise attention to herself by yelling "Help!" and running away if a stranger tries to touch her.

• Tell her never to get into a stranger's car or go into a stranger's home.

• Keep your child's identity a secret by ensuring her name is tucked away on the inside of her clothes and belongings.

How can I keep my baby safe in the sun?

Research has shown that sunburn in childhood can be very damaging, and has been linked to a higher incidence of skin cancer in later life. So it's essential to protect your baby or child's delicate skin from the sun's harmful rays at all times.

Your baby's skin is extremely delicate, and it may take only a few minutes to burn in the sun. Protect your baby or child by:

★ **keeping him in the shade as much as possible** This is especially important between 10 am and 4 pm, depending on the latitude, when damaging rays are at their strongest. Babies under six months should be kept out of the sun at all times.

★ **keeping him covered** Choose loose, cotton clothing with a tight weave, which covers limbs, and a wide-brimmed sun hat. Sunglasses that block 99 to 100 per cent of UV light are a good idea for older children.

★ **preventing him becoming overheated** Offer lots of fluids to drink to avoid dehydration.

Using a sunscreen

In addition to taking the measures above, using a sunscreen will protect your child further. Choose one specially designed for babies and children, with a sun protection factor (SPF) of 15 or greater.

★ For babies under six months, when there is not enough shade or clothing available, apply a minimal amount of sunscreen to small exposed areas of skin, such as the face and the back of the hands.

★ For older babies and children, apply sunscreen to all exposed areas of skin at least 30 minutes before going out, even on cloudy days. Reapply every two hours, or after your baby or child has been in water.

STAY COOL!
A cotton wide-brimmed hat is essential to protect your baby or child from the sun and to keep him cool during the summer months. You may have to be firm to ensure that he keeps it on, but a chin strap or ties should help.

Useful contacts

BabyCentre.com/safety/
Offers comprehensive online advice on baby and child safety.

British Red Cross
9 Grosvenor Crescent
London SW1X 7EJ
Tel: 020 7235 5454
www.redcross.org.uk

BSI (British Standards Institution)
389 Chiswick High Road
London W4 4AL
Tel: 020 8996 9001
www.bsi-global.com
Sets safety standards for British products, including toys and nursery equipment.

British Toy & Hobby Association
80 Camberwell Road
London SE5 0EG
Tel: 020 7701 7271
www.btha.co.uk
Represents the British toy market, and provides toy safety information.

Child Accident Prevention Trust (CAPT)
18-20 Farringdon Lane
London EC1R 3HA
Tel: 020 7608 3828
www.capt.org.uk
Provides useful advice about all aspects of child safety.

Children's Fire and Burn Trust
Cayzer House
30 Buckingham Gate
London SW1E 6NN
Tel: 020 7802 8464
www.childrensfireandburntrust.org.uk
Aims to promote the prevention of burns and scalds to children and aid the long-term rehabilitation of children suffering traumas of burns.

Department for Transport
Great Minster House
76 Marsham Street
London SW1P 4DR
Tel: 020 7644 8300
www.dft.gov.uk

Department of Health
Richmond House
79 Whitehall
London SW1A 2NS
Tel: 020 7210 4850
www.doh.gov.uk

European Child Safety Alliance
PO Box 75169
1070 AD Amsterdam
The Netherlands
Tel: +31 20 511 4513
www.childsafetyeurope.org
The European Child Safety Alliance is an initiative of the European Consumer Safety Association to advance child injury prevention throughout Europe.

Food Standards Agency
Aviation House
125 Kingsway
London WC2B 6NH
Tel: 020 7276 8000
www.foodstandards.gov.uk
Provides useful information on food hygiene, safety and labelling.

Foundation for the Study of Infant Deaths (FSID)
Artillery House, 11-19 Artillery Row
London SW1P 1RT
Helpline: 0870 787 0554
www.sids.org.uk/fsid/
Offers support and education to parents and professionals on reducing the risk of Sudden Infant Death Syndrome (SIDS).

NHS Direct
Tel: 0845 4647
www.nhsdirect.nhs.uk

Royal Life Saving Society UK
River House, High Street
Broom, Warwickshire B50 4HN
Tel: 01789 773994
www.lifesavers.org.uk
Promotes lifesaving skills and water safety, providing training and information.

Royal Society for the Prevention of Accidents (RoSPA)
Edgbaston Park, 353 Bristol Road
Edgbaston
Birmingham B5 7ST
Tel: 0121 248 2000
www.rospa.com
Offers general safety information, advice and training.

St Andrew's Ambulance Association
48 Milton Street
Glasgow G4 0HR
Tel: 0141 332 4031
www.firstaid.org.uk
Provides first-aid training and services in Scotland.

St John Ambulance
27 St John's Lane
London EC1M 4BU
Tel: 08700 104950
www.sja.org.uk
Provides first-aid training and services in the UK.

Index

Acknowledgments

Dorling Kindersley would like to thank Sally Smallwood and Ruth Jenkinson for the photography, and Sue Bosanko for compiling the index.

Models Joe with Mia Brookes, Arianne Shah, Hannah Hyman, Marcello with Mia and Joseph Griso, the Benveniste family, Joanna Rosenfeld with Katarina Henderson, Kofinan Agyemang, Aimee Morland, the Karamallakis family, the Wijayarajaran family, Jenny Cheng, Carla Pollard, Anna with Ben Dawson, the Lou-Fong family, Sharon with Dominic Gunn, Sophira Elliott, Rita with Robin Brown, Dynia Lawrence with Tsehay and Tasheba Lee, Maureen Lopatkin with Mia Schindler, Jenny with Baobao Cao, Yvonne with Jordan Townsend, the Reilly family.

Hair and make-up Louise Heywood, Victoria Barnes, Susie Kennett, Amanda Clarke

Picture researcher Anna Bedewell

Picture librarian Romaine Werblow

Picture credits
The publisher would like to thank the following for their kind permission to reproduce their photographs:
45: Safety 1st
All other images © Dorling Kindersley. For further information see: www.dkimages.com